Æpocalyptics

C. Derick Varn

Unlikely Books
www.UnlikelyStories.org
New Orleans, Louisiana

Fifteen Dollars US

ISBN 978-0-9988925-5-9

First Printing

Unlikely Books
www.UnlikelyStories.org
New Orleans, Louisiana

ÆPOCALYPTICS

The Order in Which They Appear

Foreword: On What Cannot Be Said

Be it gentle or harsh, the words from my mouth cannot speak enough. We—that is, the you that is
reading—   and the I—   that is—   only   know   the   smell of
day lilies   or   the cry   of   our
two-month-old niece   when   the formula   is   unwarmed. Beyond
this.   Beyond. This.   Nothing.   A   wood owl sits
in   my window,   its tuffs   may speak to me,   each feather ruffled
as a   vowel   and   my eyes   too narrow   to be prey   may be a
novel but   owl   and I   cannot   talk.   Cannot   speak
of   dead   field mice.   Cannot speak   of   day-old sex.   Cannot speak
of coffee.   Or other owls, white or plumed or brown.   As I to you.   If you do
not have   an owl   or   a niece. What. What then.   What can be known.

7

I. Late Night Like Blended Fruit

Violence: Catachresis and Catechism

Do not forget to address your fathers with
    dissonant tongues of blue flame they left you.
Do not take in vain the watering eyes which
    cry at the broken ephemera of now churning the dross.
Do not take the violence of the metaphor as
    ironic lest you want to speak through broken teeth.
Do not forget to drink freely from the milk
    of our revenge—bitter symmetry on tongue.
Do not wash the bloodied face of history as
    you approach the outmost star floating in milky black.
Do not look into the obscure origins of these
    injunctions as your will be stripped of your outer body.
Do not sever the fear from your belly, as
    it will birth your ocean and act as your raft to the shore.

Another *Ars Poetica*

Unless you engage
In the autumn saccharin
You'll know that beauty
Rots your teeth
And resists
The completed
Verse enamel

So if you battled
Out your verse
Bloodied
Vulnerable
Most definitely
Alone and
Laughing
The last
Laugh

You'll know
That the alphabet
Lied from the beginning
From the babble of
The primordial
Soup

We've always
Been Ariadne
Alone and left
For gulls to
Pick apart
And yet
We need
To have
Something

Beautiful to
Whisper to
Drunken and
Near-impotent
Lovers.

Words like church bells
creaking into still gray sky
and shattering the clouds:

a soldier in the distance
and against the horizon
two lovers, feeling each

other's mouths. Silence
in the groping, like a dentist
whose most intimate touch

is myopic and cuts the top
of the palate. Rifle fire
over the hill toward

Dalmatia. The murdered
dead over the hills where
goats mull over the grass:

there is not a creature
left unshivering. Visitations
are mistaken for signs.

Apocaplytics

Too many lattes for memories
to flow easily, but not whisky
to take it straight. Remembering

sweat from the swelter as
the Twin Towers fell: my girlfriend
in Johnstown, but the phones

nothing but distant static;
after everyone stopped crying
two young women kissed

on the couch as we watched
a movie to avoid the repeat
of the news. I once read

the way the cells can mutate:
growing over fecund, and
exploding. No Jasper Johns

canvas blank enough, stark
enough for the memory of
a woman stripped to bra

and panties, crying at
a party the turn of the
last millennium, the weight

of zeros hitting her core
as she had partially stripteased
away to the future in the

champagne haze. One wants
to see so much. I have been
to the remains of the cave

on Patmos: nothing but
historical markers and rocks.
My father, my king, my

fear of sex addiction. Like
a cicada's carapace, I woke
with a lover between me

and another man that New
Year's Eve. When I return
to places where the night

stays dark, I see myself emerging
with a soft exoskeleton, sore
from all the changes I am.

Learning How to Fall

The glittered dust   in the carpet
                    is   all the   more breathtaking as I   stare
face down against the floor   I   press against   the
                    streaked   plum purple   of
            my   fractured   rib   to   trip
        to travel   down   into the railing   and   have
            your blood pulse   each   square inch of skin
illuminated   by   a   floodlight   of   a   heart-beat
                    footing lost   likened   to   turbulence
tossed about   I am vacated   and   vacant   The   groceries   never make it
to   the   second   floor   the inertia
calibrated   to   pull   apart   the side   like
a   pelican   feeding   her   young   on
her   own   blood
vulning   herself
a   myth   no doubt   but   potent   my   lungs
        ache   from   lying   like   damaged
        goods   here   I   remember
        watching   a   brown pelican   dive
towards   the coastline outside   of   Tybee   Island
        a grace   a   downward   blossoming
into   the   ocean   Its   hollow   bones
could   shatter   against   the   wrong   wave
        Now   as   I   lie   still   on   the
stairs
                    to   my   apartment   pecked   apart
by   gravity   I only   wish   I   knew
        the exact   angle   between   flight   and
falling

16

In not writing
Those particularly
Well-referenced
Anecdotes of
Our days: the
Endless pantomime
Of voiceless "I"s
Looking intently
At the grizzled
Beard of their
Father far in
A past too long
Forgotten. To
Say "we," like
We watch the
Koi dart across
A pond, is to
Assume too
Much. We
Know the
Taste of our
Own blood
But only
Vaguely care
For the copper
And coffee grind
Taste of
Others.

Things in Themselves

"You get tragedy where the tree, instead of bending, breaks." —Wittgenstein

On the day my lung collapses,
deflates and pops in the slow
air of the red-apple autumn, we
see how much we value life—
the simple caveat contracts
in the shifting sunlight, estrangement
lifting into contagion like
a semi-truck carving the
interstate with brakes giving
way as it rolls into steel
rails and flattens sumac
in the valley. Crushed by
the terrible math of wheels
half-seared into the highway,
despite the doggerel of lonely
atoms, out of sync with
the unending Styrofoam
models from childhood
science classes tossed in the
rubbish heaps. Pebbles
break into an even smaller
kaleidoscope of detritus.
So where is the human in
the trodden things that
I see as I gasp for one
more cool breath.

I learned:
time scrubs the
palette clean, stale
crumbs around
the lips, the taste
of vinegar and
coffee grounds.
Dumpster diving

on a Saturday night .
in cool evening
air, electric growl
of cicadas beyond
passing cars. Jerry's
hand shivers,
illuminating welts
and tumors in
street light.

I stare into
chrome bumpers, watch
the sky tense
like a knotted muscle.
I swallow the bread
crust. The next day,

his hands stiffen and chill.
His two-dollar necktie
hangs from his
shirt, his eyes empty
as a broken icebox.

What I remember then:
Hog's blood from
my grandfather's hands,
light glaring into the bathroom
as he scrubs
with rutted soap.
The air steeps in pig
stink and white lightning.

I still hear the squeals
sliding from the pig's slit
throat. That night, Grandfather
and I have bacon.

To both ghosts I'd like to say:
How does the body
rise up against the
lack of bread?
When the body
dries like fruit
left in the sun,
how does one
learn the lack
of lack? Frequent
bleeding, tender gums,
a slit throat. What
if the sky is falling
like a bloated belly
collapsing inward?
What could be said?

What I still cannot say:
Confusion of Tense. This blur.
This hunger. Blood. Meat.
Pork shoulder. AIDS.
Teeth. This Future. Teeth.
This Past. Teeth. This Sweet.
This Sweet Nothing. This.

Two   in   the   morning
                    his   mind soaks   infomercials
                and   ennui   when   stale
coffee   lingers
            like   the   smell
                            of sex and thoughts   mingle
        with death
                        then   a plastic-faced   woman with
        juicer   attacks   a   medley
of fruits: grapes
                    burst   apples break   kiwis dance
spinning blades
                            flash   on   the
                                omnicolor screen.

                Perhaps   it is the   pulp
turning   into juice
                    losing   its   solid   status
which invokes   particles of   woman
                        passing   through
space   like   a   blown-out   kiss.

The plush velour of his   recliner
                    rubs   the   small of his
back and he   ambles
            into the kitchen   to   void
his   head of the salt taste of their   blending: all   of   her
                                            drowning   in
                a   few   swallows
                of   orange   juice   with
a splash   of   vodka   then   cool   sleep.

Interrogative

Do you dream of vultures
picking at the roadside deer,
stripping it down to the framing
and inner lace like a negligee
in autumn? Do you take
the bullet trains to the edge
of the world, watch oceans
fall into the abyss of stars

despite the impossible
cosmology? Do you know
the continental drift, pulling
the plates apart from their
marriage, a slow spat
between the ashen, rocky
lovers until they crash
into a new partner?

Do you see the trains
coming in from Russia
to Paris, across the Asian
tundra? Do you know
where we wait for each
other? Do you know my
ex-wife? Do you know
the ache of scavenging?

Do you see the caribou
carcass in the distance
buzzing alone? Do you
know the tracks we called
sweetie and *darling* do
not end? Do you know
they can keep going?
Do you want to save

me from this wandering?
Do you want to keep me
like a locket, close to your
heart but covered in metal?
Do you care that this is not
about you? Do you see the
sky? Do you know it's empty?
Do you care? Do you?

Doubting

There is a slip to slip into
But one wonders if break beats
Break faster than glass. There
Are many famous poets younger
Than me. The slipping moves
Up the ladder. Repeated images
In the codex: rotted incisors,
Blood in alcohol, dusted cow
Bones, clouds in aperture.
Wry comments lining the halls:
Once I tried to write about what
Beauty was and all I got was
Three ribbons made of lousy
T-shirt. Once I tried to write
About you: a you, the you,
A thousand mock trails filled
With under-written and vague
Ghosts dredged up from the
Deep muck of dead girlfriends,
Friends in wayward cabbage
Patches in backyards sometime
In the mid-1980s. When I met
Beauty once, I broke the syntax
For it. Some people say things
Like *make love* as code for sex,
But I say *sex* and mean coldness:
Something one does not long
To touch, something one wants
To watch live past yourself. All
That silly etcetera; all that miasma
Of miserable parties lingering
Just a little longer than one
Should. The bar is closing:
We came this far to have
Nothing to say. We came.
At least. There are no puns
In punishment, and nothing
More masochistic than a poet

Doubting. Might as well hog-tie
Him with words, whip her with
Some dangling clause. There is
Always too much you for one
Play session. There always more
Browned teeth, blood in whisky,
Malted iron on the tongue. We
Are running. Running out of words.

The Floodgates of the Pronoun

For A.K.

Break in with the I
and cut to the you
with all its invariable
slippage, new
like monsoon
mud smears on
pants legs.
There is you—
the you that
poem chats
with idly.
You breaking
new fragments.
Again, the I.
The utterance:
the car alarm
in the distance.
The image that
lingers too long
off the establishing
shot. Generic
like a paper cup.
Functionless like
a simile. You,
sound, You,
affectation,
You, body
without smell,
without the
heady perfume
of stale cigarettes
or the overstay
of cardamom
on the skin.
All too vast,
All too full
of fondness,

All. The I.
I breaks into
new vases,
shards collecting
in a heap
near the tracks
where the I
lived once,
where the I
diagrammed
sentences
from German,
where the I
dreamed in
Esperanto.
Where the
I mourned
the hurried
rain and
tangled hair,
pragmatic
enough to be
sad and thaw
the raw meat
of the heart
just enough
to brown the
edges. There
all is sun,
bright light
where the you
sleeps. Negation
of negation.
Loss of referent.
The I breaks,
rebuilds, installs
storm windows,
cracks next storm,
rebuilds again.
Learns to speak
the foreign tongue
of air. The I

breaks better.
Breaks with
beauty, grateful
for a chance
amongst the pot
shards. To be
re-kilned, kindled
and cooled
in night air.
To take the blank
invitation. To
start again.

I. Inertia

My stomach shifts as my girlfriend sweats,
whispers about locked lips with a cross-
dresser she met in Savannah. I-75 North

propels us toward the mountains. Dragonflies
spread across the windshield, pus spectral
like the glare across Atlanta, or like the dew dripping

from wilting lilacs. She continues. I breathe,
a being in motion with a 1967 Colt .45 hiding
in the glove box. The safety broken as we hit

seventy barreling toward Chattanooga. Words
push forward, like a lily rising through kudzu.
A brake squeals. The car stops. I reach for the dash.

II. Friction

Motion erotic, abstract glaring
through weeds.   She may
taste like cinnabar. She may
drip like the ice of Mars.   I
pull my hand away. Her words,
washable as each could easily
into questions. The bullets lie
she mouths *forgive me.* Hazard
in an abyss, the dragon eyes of
wheelers   glare as I taste the
rubbing between the there
of headlights
say *his lips*
say *his hips*
taste bile
machine
turn
dormant as
lights strobe
eighteen-
burn
and not-there.

My Life with the Demons of Language

for Michael Palmer

Language on fire: Leningrad no longer,
    one specter replaced   to haunt another.
The words have content: Saint Petersburg
    alight over the Neva River.   Poets
proliferate in the lean times   words to chew on
    fills the mouth   and bloats the tongue
like thick bread.   Syntax is non-operational.   Who
speaks for the human   in the theory of color.   The
    statues of Engels   lay by the water
        half-sunken in silt.
There is a man staring back   with half a face,
      eyes like black holes.   Language
is the lie   we tell ourselves: Words
gave light in the cave   the shadows move in.
      There is silence at Nyenschantz :
invisible graves   where Peter the German   took the fort
    in the deeper quiet of snow.   So much
forgotten in the renaming.   General Yudenich marched in the
    city of three revolutions.   Then an.   Language on fire.
The Aurora is a museum now.   A philosopher talks
    to himself about a theory of color.   The poet about a
theory of sound.   The Red Army about dialectics.   The chatter
of   ages.   The angels are mute
    Because there are   demons   who speak.
Because the syntax is parsed.   Flames on the Volga. Flames
    on the Neva.   Flames on the pronoun.   Amputated
legs of white army soldiers in   retreat.   The old name
    comes back.   There are no (or many) theories.
Too many fossil negotiations.   Too many migratory words

Demarcation Poem

"If we are uncritical we shall always find what we want: we shall look for, and find, confirmations, and we shall look away from, and not see, whatever might be dangerous to our pet theories."
—Sir Karl Popper, *"The Poverty of Historicism"*

So we can give
you a problem:

The New Year's
rotting hairs released
in a slurry of gray
and brown. Navel-
gazing doesn't
tell you much
about yourself
except that
your eyes
can't peer past
lint into viscera.

If "A" is for Apollonian,
"D" for Dionysian,
then Nietzsche
botched variables
of the equation.
If you are searching
for answers, have
breakfast first, or
the truth won't
tell. "Nonsense,"

you say. The
divination of
hair in the sink
or mapping
of veins, no
more scientific
than palmistry.

If "D" is for Death
and "L" is for Life,
then the symbolism
is too blatant. We're
still struggling
for meaning's
lines to be
clearer, to cut
away the dead
weight, which
may be life
itself.

Meta-commentary

So much has been said
about contemporary disorientation
and the loss of authoritative voice, whose baritone
no longer muffs out the various dangling participles,
and thus with the death of the author, who collectively
lies supine and half-dissected upon the autopsy table,
and, let us not be remiss to mention, the hemorrhaging
of the I incised and splayed, and the way poets approach
language like a policeman sneaking up on a soldier
who fondled a woman in a bar, the metaphor
spins out of control as does a sentence
that becomes self-aware and dazed.
Everything is, of course, a lie,
a footnote to some off-color
wheelbarrow.

What we remember:
Jacob's ladder
folding into itself,
Bethel pruned by
Klezmer guitarists
with Mohawks,
the letters of Torah
mixed with the dust
of earth and stars.

Seventy rungs
of desire, each
one a little more
distant from
the previous,
each vibrating
with honey
on razor wire:

Jacob breathes
in want. Half-
drowns. The
seraphim
move like
coupling teens
in a parking deck.

The ladder bends
further over Haran's
sycamores, above
Esau's head,
and arches over
Leah and Rachel.

We know
of no ladder
to heaven:
only to want,
curved
like a hip
over Canaan.

Being in Time

"The past in memory, like the future in our imagination, is more beautiful than the present. Why? Because only the present has a true shape in our mind, it's the only image of truth, and all truth is ugly."
—*Giacomo Leopardi,* Zibaldone di pensieri

The truth is not ugly. It is. Take a given
moment, parse it into bits, and look at
the rolled bones. You'll see an exotic
ending spreading toward infinity. Even
failure has erotic overtones. So hold the
following to be self-evident, even the moist parts.

The negotiated version: small fragments
of various dispositions, note the absence
of color, note the motionless light, note
the veering from the subject periodically.
The gas heater laments the lack of cold
feet. No need to lift my own eyelids.

The nominal sense of shame: the way
the blue eyes turn down, the incessant
humming, the slow and obtuse turning
away, the shallow midnight movement,
the way hipsters curl their beards, the fear
of being found by hounds, other hyperbole.

Meanness heightens one's discrimination:
my ex-wife turns off the television set, hugs
me too tightly before I get on the plane. So
many poets write about the slow lingering
of divorce. Its pageant of billings, half-fights
whole-wars, despondent breaking apart.

The obligatory nostalgia: the pained heave
of narrative. Each story with its beginning,
middle, end. No matter the order. The truth
is self-evident. The truth is in the space between.
The truth is that we are all asunder in our days.
The truth is not beauty. Not ugliness. It is.

Stasis

"To function, memory requires a fixed, stable object"
—*Giacome Leopardi*, Zibaldone di pensieri

Ellipses indicate omissions. Syntax:
a slippery slope. Piles of magazines
are rubrics, small devotions. The fogged
peaks of the mountains outside my window
line my pleasure. The closest one comes
to clarity is oxtails rustling in wind.

At the bottom of things: glass and blood
wash out of your hair. Speak in tongues
until the flames spout forth. Colons
tell you there is more to come. Calling
your name at night, sweet decline, long
goodbye. Sheet metal, bottles, and bones

kick the lies out of your mouth. Trace
of one before. Fire for your eyes. Entice
a hand to help you out of the wreckage. Entice
a memory to resonate on your lips. Take
your car and drive it home in pieces. Hard
to remember: resurrect the way I call your

name. Tell the truth; it wouldn't help
anyway. Keep the glass out of your hair.
Blue and gold lights churn down the river.
If we spoke of what happened, we'd have
to remember the bits and pieces. Sometimes
bad weather follows good people. Sometimes.

Limitations: Tone to Tone

Much has been said on thunderous silence:
the gradual unmooring of the voice you hear,
long half-drowned in the inky past, and if the
scream you have choked back, kicked open
your lips and drank the greenish air. There

is more to say on nothing than can be said:
someone is feeding sparrows, someone is
becoming the small world, and sparrows
fly to become nations, and nations become
noise, and noise, the parataxis.   Like a

hawk, voice wants to ride a mechanical
horse into heaven, break the harmony
of the planets, and place the notes in new
order, place the notes into a chorus only
silence hears. The silence knows how

to rumble the bones, how to cut to the
quick, how to feed sparrows, to end
the end of chirping, how to unsing
the national anthems, how to take
away the hymn of a land that was
never ours in the first place.

Composition in Motion

For L.N.

"The mystical is not how the world is, but that it is."
—Ludwig Wittgenstein, Tractatus Logico-Philosophicus

Last night, I almost choked
on the smoke that drenched my
shirt. The remainder of
women tensely woven together
through limbs twisting
in music or wind. I almost
evaporated in wisps
engrossed

    in the philosophy of moment
    I can't speak, can't rattle on
    for once there is no new silence
    no odious babble about nothing
    much

                  Nothing new
                  the thin curve of
                  the road like tendrils
                  in shrouding streetlights

      On the radio, static, then
      as I change channels:
      Doctors and Tutsis
      building a road—callous
      hands in Burundi

                  something inhuman
                  rising from the steam
                  of the street—

     Nothing but the slow churn
     of an oak branch into the cool
     shingles, erupting the complex
     roof lines and soon coaxing
     rooms into thick rain

unpacked paradigms of bodies
fueled by scotch and gin
slip to the left—herd-stained
and heated with compact
muscular sinew

a marginal mother
digs the brush road
her baby coated in sweat
she knows that a hospital
will come

I can't speak for others
In fractal and fragment
What is the logic of breakage?

The glare on the asphalt
animates like a Ouija board
arcane markers in the memory
and strange dashboard
refractions

I don't dance, nor could I
watch myself watching
the eyes of others

I think and tremble
I cannot speak
Of women of motion
Women in motion
Of mourning wails

The perpetual push
As I sip lager at too
Late an hour

the road, the signposts,
Whatever the fauna shows
Of itself in the rearview

Where shall I wonder

thread-bare	I can't speak	the wonder	the mandrake void	I am not
syntax	highway swerving	tremulous hand of a mourning mother		the blurring
the nervous look	self-aware	pluming	crescendo	well-lit places
reflected	on the radio, static	tense,	coughing,	breakable
Where shall I	arcane women	what is	the logic	I can't speak
I don't dance	what is	late	and	blending
Odious chorus	prattling hours	in rearview	tendrils twining	in motion
Everything	perilous	all journeys	nothing	chopped
Into early	inaudible	hours	of	morning

II. Like History, Like a Pasolini Film

Erosion

Although you can hardly avoid it,
it's hard to be human. Always slipping
in and out of the perpetual intermission
between lonely longing and the scum
at the bottom of the sink. You expect
that you will not die of grief as you sob
and masturbate, but nothing's certain.
Your memory akin to blurred pixels,
or soil sorting into ever-neater strata
of forgotten debris. You're always
claiming the high road as it washes
away: feet stuck in drying mud
and pressing downward, inward,
where lunch dates aren't forgotten
and men can stare at sunflowers
without miasmas of useless hours.

Similes Against Sex

Like the flutter of birds against fir needles
when a tiger mauls a hunter against a backdrop
of monochrome snow. Like the wheels of a bicycle
spinning, spinning while the rider cannot stop
without plowing deep into the pavement. Like
an orchid blooming on demand, out of sync
with its season, petals half wilted. Like night's
heavy winds that rip down branches and pull kinks
out of matted hair. Like the hoarse moans of coeds
fucking so hard the stereo cannot muffle each
breath. Like a picked-over crab left dead
and covered in high-tide sand as the beach
recedes into the ocean. Like cauliflower
molded. Like touching ice. Like waiting hours.

Aesthetic Theory

after talking to A. about Dario Argento

A philosopher once said, "Beauty is the promise
of happiness—true or false?" The phrasing like
a poorly written test question, but dangling

modifier all the more profound. So if this
is the case: what beauty is in the lingering
of maggots in the ceiling while ballet

students dine in a movie where murders
are enacted with the director's hands? Does
the shadow contrast with the promise?

Do truth and beauty dangle each
other from the rafters, each lovingly tying
the knots of the kikkou until bound

and struggling for balance or release?
My friend reminds me how the camera
cuts away at the moment of death—

like the jarring of the eye in shock.
Voyeur to the promise. But it is
a friend who tells me this, all

in all, far beyond my hearing,
and I realize that perhaps the lingering
of the conversation is a promise kept.

Erosion 2

Feeling the mattress
tense like an overextended
leg beneath me. My
graying hair all over the
sweat-stained pillow;
all I can think about
is Augustine's secular
city: we can take the damned
free-will we deserve.
The end of the day
with happy-hour grace
as if happiness were
drunk, vomiting on
the nearest promenade.
Somewhere I read
if you hold something
warm, its easier to get
a date. The cold feels
good blistering my face:
I am not alone, but I am
who brought me here
when the morning
hung heavy on
the chest.

Feed Your Wolves

I. yetzer tov

The aged, worn hymnal
near my bed was given
to me by Grandfather—

the split leather and pages
yellowed like coffee-stained
teeth to guide me in singing

praise like the Methodist
I never have been: Once,
my grandfather told me

that in every man two
wolves lie, one black
with greed and anger,

the other white with
bravery, both willing to
bloody their muzzle

but nipping at each
other's throat at the heart
of every man. I asked him

which one would win,
and he told me the one
you feed. But now my

grandfather's dust is mixed
with Georgia clay, I know
that feeding is only so

easy; give a strip of meat
to one, the other snaps
the scraps, growling, both

growing in sinew and jaw, feasting
on yourself as you lay supine.

II. yetzer ra

My mother's lupus gnaws
on her face from within,
and I watch her hand shake
as she lifts her tea to her lips,

parched as they are with
skin leathering with years.
My partner's hands quake
when her heart speeds

up I would rip open
the sky to settle her nerves,
smooth the neurons, unknot
the muscles, the heart.

An ex-lover and I talk,
between grief and grievance,
not hinting that the almost
daughter we treat as ghost

seems real despite stillbirth. She
could not speak of it as a child
but neither could she not,
instead leaving an offering to Jizo

Buddha for safe passage
between the life that could
have been and might be. Pain
between prosody and prosaic,

I feed the wolves, needing both
sets of teeth for the task of loving,
as if one could choose between
the love one wants and the love

one has, no matter how the waste
wilts, one needs both jaws sharp.
Between the mouths, I cannot
bring myself to toss the hymnal

into a fire, watch it curl into ash,
then nothing, nor sing the shape notes.

Festival of Lights

My friend burns candles
for Diwali, materializing
flame, desperately seeking
symmetry in the dead

of the afternoon amongst
shades. Her brown skin
like roasted barley against
light, brighter than diamonds

or street flares. Listening to Iggy
Pop's "The Passenger" on a digital
jukebox in late 1999: time
substitutes for space. Erasure.

Palimpsest like plums boiled
to pulp and drying for candies
on a screen. We sang then
as if our drunken voices

could shank Ravana in
the back alley. We sang
like it was a hymn to Prozac
and Shiva ringing through

the greasy spoon. Sound
substitutes for space. Setting
itself in like bursting firecrackers
in July. She touched my arm

gently when we stopped,
light contrasting our then-
young faces with wrinkled,
dry, dark, and cool time.

Sometimes Gray Bodies

"The ruined world is mainly gray but the occasional flash, like epauletted blackbird you remember, is all the sweeter now for its rarity."
—Bin Ramke, "The Ruined World"

I.

Bridge (brig), n.

1. any structure of wood, stone, brick, or iron raised to afford
convenient passage over a river, pond, lake, railroad, ravine, or
any other obstacle.

Panoramic:
gray: sky, gray.
gray.
inward,
washes legs
coral,
red kelp
skin foam together.
across the stunning

the beach bleeds
Sand, gray. Water,
Yet zooming
the surf
and hues blend: blue
silvery scales,
and ochre
A hermit crab squirms
monochrome.

I approach. When it's time to walk,
we walk. Lucent sun against water.
A dock, bridge to nowhere:

where the sea bounces
driftwood on its chest.
The brined planks scratch

the soles of my feet. My
brother clicks knuckles
against thighs with wave rhythm.

Once we reach the end,
the salt mists our faces.
A gull swoons overhead.

In the beginning,
words spoken through cracked
teeth. I stood over my brother, holding
small wounds that laced my
arm. I extended my hand, bruised the
color of rotted wood. He
retracts—automatic—as if I am lifting my
fist to crush him against the beachhead.

The Sea, always　　　　　　　　　　　*reckoning: a chest*
that rises and falls　　　　　　　　　*with long, patient*
pants. The brown-haired　　　　　*girl complements the*
ocean's contours,　　　　　　　　　*legs like the tides:*
escalating and　　　　　　　　　　　*slimming to shore,*
flesh fluid like　　　　　　　　　　　*water splashing*
on my feet.

For a while there is something to build
on: My brother glances backward;
his wife skims through surf, picking shells.

His hair, longer then,
frayed edges from
wear. I turned to Mother,
huddled. I, a tide between
two thoughtless shores.
My stomach sunk from
the blood lines on his jaw, left by
my knuckles, when

Nothing revolutionary　　　　　　*in touching a hip*
yet the clammy slick　　　　　　　*flesh on flesh*
keeping the hordes　　　　　　　　*of Puritans at bay*

The tide pounds and cascades
along the coast like a cheap deck
of cards, crashing into the dock

and spraying mist in our eyes
until the glare is the gleaming.
He says, "Has Father spoken to you?"

Wind, arctic,
cool freezes
that something
knows as her
the sea.

ancient, the
water, bodies
my lover
arms become

II.

2. in electricity, a device employed to measure resistance,
frequencies, etc., by comparing the effect of the unknown element
with that of a known or standard element in a circuit.

He hit mother. His eyes
      white-traced with red like
        a shark's teeth on
           the Atlantic floor. My fist,
              a harpoon, equally blank. Blue
           lights flashed on the vinyl siding.
        Sirens screamed. Police held back
     my stepfather, his face so
tight it bled.

His hands flank his cropped hair.
At 16, both father and Samson,
he turns from the sea

and looks back at his lover.
"He's not my . . ." I reply.
"You know what I mean,"

He snaps his head back.
To escape the danger
of being unscathed

Sunlight was brighter   *than famed*
bridge blooming over   *a small salt marsh*
sea blew me kisses   *delicately*
like little prayers   *or unprayers*
to the trace   *scooped out*
blankets   *something close*
enough   *to love*

In the machinery of the forest,
my brother all bones, his
flesh grinded by moss-furred
boulders. He lays still underwater.
When I lift him out,
freezer-burned, and eyes
gray like a trout on a
hook. When paramedics cut vines
to cross the creek, they see me
naked and shivering above a
bundle of flesh and
swaddling clothes.

The wood creaks as
I sit down, skipping
shells into the waves.

After his wedding, we swam until
        our legs were pruned. His honey-
            moon had sunk into the distance
                the day before. We had spoken
        no words for weeks.
    I wished his wife luck with
the bulge in her belly.

III.

3. in dancing, a bending backwards to touch the floor.

"Is it true why you don't talk to him?"
He sits beside me, stiff-backed as I turn
jellyfish. He says

"Did you really kiss a man?"
A wave crashes, barnacles
fending off the ocean.

People are a landscape   *Declarative yet secret*
proximities, each too   *close and anonymous*
like the lover whose   *name you forget*
but whose stale smell   *won't wash off*

We embraced like twining sea
weeds when he limped out of
prison. I could not crack a sound.

Of course, I could be Judas-tongued
and answer "no," lying like a starfish
on the shore. Instead, I stand straight

and kiss his fuzzy cheek, then smile.
Walking off, I expect him to whisper "faggot,"
but he is quiet as I step off onto the sand

Her breath is   *rich like the*
smell of scallops   *and her back*
arches. She   *gyrates the*
ocean, slams   *into the jagged*
coastline, leaves   *skeletons of*
clams on rocks   *like the dot-to-*
dot blemishes   *on her arms.*

IV.

4. in lovemaking, the arch of the back, or the curve of the lip.

My mother shrinks like coral
when he is near, but his tentacles
remain lower and his fist loose.
My brother, shark; myself, shark.
The world is only water now that
he has his own daughter to watch.

The wings in the spine,　　　　　*struggling to kiss and*
remember that men　　　　　*love lips of all kinds,*
mouths move, gnaw　　　　　*the tongues into one.*

The tide still droning,
I hear his steps behind me.
The echoes pound

semen, sweat,　　　　　*and latex graying*
on clean sheets as　　　　　*waves devour the*
dock planks.　　　　　*We lie together*
in black and　　　　　*white froth. The*
tide sucks　　　　　*away all color*
as she puts on　　　　　*her panties.*

infinite waves
as he tries to walk beside me.
Air deep as nerves.

Nothing left
but stunning
chiaroscuro.
Nothing, but

Like History

Broken men are an abundant
resource, verdant like spring
kudzu and as useful, filling hours
with primal clay forged of brow

sweat and ephemera that clogs
the gutters of September. This minor
landscape, still gray and bungled
by natural design, blurs in focus.

Entire nations swell and bloat in
the memory, start to smell of
their pox-marked cities, sand
castles washed away on

artificial beach. I walk through all
this, like Hansel on a shining path
with his guerrilla armaments, so
much like a bloodied dream, my

shoulders tense and wet from
the pricks of malicious rain. Ours
is not a beautiful age: whatever
that means is unclear, and no

age is particularly aware. So there
is this ocean blooming red algae
that chokes the fish and feelings.
The density of air can crack the bone,

sap the marrow of its fat; my thoughts
rip each apart, caught in the depressurized
cabin. Labor is the hardest won, unchosen
leisure leaves the muscles brittle:

the monochrome possibilities leave the lens
range narrowed like a razor, the fading of
color sharpens the edges and blunts the
force residing before one war and after

another. No surprise. I will lay in the
submissive position, waiting for the arc
of the fist. I will breathe saltwater and
smoke thick as rancid butter, sputter

my blood thick as concrete. The mortar
that holds it all together mixed of the
mal-shaped minds of men. I'll listen to
magpies and watch women in fuck-me

pumps walk by the boardwalk. We all
must mend our own spines. Heart beating
like a breeze blowing down open stairs.
There is no shortage of broken men.

Transgression

In fall, the red and yellow,
come memories of snow, melting
to thickly crushed ice. When

you get this message, I will have
long since been high above
the earth, jet-legged into

another time and place. I
woke up on her floor on New
Year's Day at noon, she in

her bed in the tiny Korean
apartment: bras scattered
apart, half-empty water

glasses, workbooks
half-graded. Why do I tell
you? The moment

I broke, my former wife
on another continent: all
too prosaic. The bough

bends in the typhoon;
I slip in snow and limp
into the slurry, but not

then. Only warmth.
The drifts of snow melt away.
Now I winter in the desert

and the tile floors in
Mexico too cold, too hard
for sleep. We break the

days apart to handle stillness.
I hear she is in Scotland now.
You are where you are too:

she was too drunk, and I,
too sad. We just talked
the next day and drank

again. Desert cold is dry,
brittle without the glimmer
and shine. I am away now,

away from the peach frost
of Georgia, corpses dead
ladybugs. The winter rain

which freezes branches You
are not there either. Who are
you now? Black ice, these

memories, blended into a
slush, the likes of which we
fall, dark yet warm. Still.

Extinction Catechism

Q: What is the light of the world to come?
A: Dreams of the omnicolor wings of black birds beating over the distant waters, the radio spires of cities sunken like the aged dreams of children.

Q: What is the crown of his glory?
A: The tree of life has many deadening branches, the flora and fauna hanging like limp leaves dwindling down into past's forest floor.

Q: What is the language of perfection?
A: There is no human story for a whale calf, heavy-bodied down into the muck that bubbles up at the bottom of the world.

Q: What is the work of creation?
A: The silence of earthen hills, the larvae-cleaned bone, and the gleaming of the split seed.

Q: What is justification?
A: The vixen breathes heavy with matted fur in the spring rain, dross hanging about her head in the dusk.

Q: What is repentance unto life?
A: Let it dive into the pre-Cambrian wastes, break down into the eukaryotic, until the amino acids that bind and break into the crystallized shards of carbon.

Q: What is the world without end?
A: Silence.

Like a Pasolini Film

Even love poems have their violence:
The returning golden-rod glow of the sun
drying the fall, tufts of grass browning
on the highway, beneath the Ford pickup
where I held you, plastic lining of the truck
bed pressing on our thighs, indenting and
scraping the skin until our blood droplets

half-mingled from the rash we
mutually granted ourselves. Sleeping,
I dream of a graying grizzly bear running
at me, running with maul open. I eying him
with a pump-action shotgun until
my stomach knotted into something
akin to a heart. The scent of oak,

pine, and sawgrass filling my
nostrils. In the future, New York
girls would inhabit the dreams,
concrete limping toward the Hudson,
where all winds come with seismic
roar, and Georgia pick-ups will

float away, but for the now, there
is you, mosquitos mixing our blood,
and a coyote baying outside in humid
rutting of the summer night.

Lilting Until the Wake Is Over

I stare into a mirror, trace the
bloodlines in my eyes
twisted by shower-steam:

Death coils in the light between
abysses, between memory's
cedar roots. In fragments
in my peripheral vision. Each glint
burns the retina like lipstick traces
on a collar. Each spectral smile
obscures the hope of seeing

the arch of moonlit walks. A Book
of Common Prayer's ruffled edges.
The small of my lover's back as I
trace the edges of the flesh. A condom
wrapper lying on the floor
like a god's cocoon.

Looking back at myself, as my
kitten licks water between
toes—coarse as sandpaper—
she mews as the veins around
Iris spread into the glass and
around the basin. Fluorescence
splaying into winged glimmers—

Each flash sings in whispers
only a short while.   *Soon,*
voices will be weighted
to hoarseness. Soon, the spark
firing the tenor will drop
into baritone, drop
into bass, and,
maybe, into silence.

Sitting, shooting spitballs at near
cloudless sky, hoping the atmospheric
clearance slips one into God's eye.
Endless hours spent wondering
about the empty sky. I tell myself

there is a story: a young man
trips into love with an alien. He
meets her in a chat room sipping
on stale coffee, black without
sugar. Later, he discovers that she

has no form, no body, only
light and sound. This complicates
things greatly, but as he sleeps
she enters him gently, rocks
his chest as he sleeps, inhabits

his breath, known and unknown.
Ten years later, some police find
him, breathing shallow, muttering
sweet, sad nothings to himself,
bedroom dusted with old skin flakes,

cat hair. Then her pushing out,
one big shutter, then he stammers
for love, not oxygen, as light drips
out of his mouth dimly. He lives
without her, hacks with his cough

into that sky. That is what love
is, you may say. What do you
know? It is afternoon, the sky
is clear, the air slicks the chest
with a brine of a coming storm.

Slippage

Nothing is about what anyone deserves:
foot to foot, the precarious lumber
through snow and the ice sheet
beneath, the off-kilter
horizon lines, and I stare.
No difference between
gleam and sky. The answer
can always be *no* in any
question of worth: sadness
forms the outline of the day,
basks in the sun which seems
higher than the sky, higher than
space, but the memory of
her voice brings proximity.
One can say that the crunch
of snow is akin to love:
purple prose melting beneath
galoshes. I slip, reach out
for the space where I wish
a woman's brown hand
would catch me, and catch
myself in the dazzle
of the guardrail. Muddled
syntax of the body: I miss
her and the ground,
trudge forward, half-limping
like a boy from the shame
of puberty, and take comfort
that, even in absence, I move
forward with the ore
of lingered voices. No question of
worth: raw palms, sprained
ankle, my mouth chapped,
the words won't stay, but
my heart trumpets down
the warmth that memory
supplies. No distance
can stop me from dredging
frozen oceans and finding
apoplectic sobbing turning
to heated joy.

Sitting in the park, I see black birds
pick apart a flattened sparrow,
tufts of feathers tower out
of the beginnings of visible
bone. I can't help but

remember. This narrative intrusion
does not go unnoticed. Memory
likes verse and birds acting oracle
to other dead birds. The move
is obvious because memory
fades like a firefly larva

growing fat on fruit
before the crab apples fall
to the ground. I am forgetting
the point, but the birds continue
eating. I think this poem is for

a woman who lives far away. Too
far to be a one-night stand, wayward
flesh missed mostly in letters. I read
somewhere that poetry is the remnant
of courtship rites. We learned to speak

first to lie, then to forget, but we learned
to rhyme to remember, and share a bed
with another woman or man of the tribe.
That is what they say, but I don't know:
the glutted crows call to me.
They don't want to share, just want
me to know. They didn't kill the sparrow

but ate it anyway.   There are mountains
in the distance of the park, sitting like
gossips in the Mexican desert just beyond
the city. The peaks remind me of
driving through Colorado, but mountains
are more dried from the sun here and
stare more blankly in their blandness.

There is so much that runs together
like mixed soil: sand, silt, and rot.
To the woman, I hope she is sitting
somewhere thinking about birds.
Thinking about past lovers, and
the awkwardness of words.
May the distance erode like
desert abrading the mountains.

More Light than Heat

I. lux ex tenebris

No hay pura luz
        I have set out to worship,
day-broken by ritual motions, and in the lost
minutes, be saved.
            ni sombra en los recuerdos.
Catholic grandmother whispers of a world
      broken. But I always wonder, from
what?
      Es tarde, tarde. Y sigo.
Rough sketches in broken Spanish. Half-formed
        Gaelic.   This part
of the religious urge is impenetrable:
        Beyond the kindling,
there are matins and novenas:
        fragments of Neruda, stale lipstick,
           the eastern horizon, where
the beloved body, reclining in her ease,
        dreams of flight. She would make
love in the pews of a Baptist church. This empty signifier.
        Winged light, angel of neon.
   Bright red neon crosses, the mission district.
el día suspendido como un puente entre sombras
        I would whisper Neruda to her, but
yearn to hum Lorca. *Odio mi cuerpo*
      even on a woman, the body is male. The ritual
breaking fast. The end of Lent. I do not celebrate
        these things. Prayers
are too light, and warmth. That alone. Prayers
      are to nothing, but maybe sometimes
to her.

II.   lucus a non lucendo

At the point of disbelief:
                    heat mimics the cold burn,
both clear and distorting.   There
                              are halo effects:
distortions of light. The way memory
functions half like a recorder, half like
            the recorded.
                    No hay deber del poeta
one could say to Neruda,
                    to she who is now an image
clear and bright, snow blinding,
                                    cold to the touch
even of memory. To her I would say
                    El remanso de tu boca
bajo espesura de besos.
                    There are not even neon
angels here. No imperial impulse
            toward the body. Nothing.
                          But the weight of light
            without heat.

I wanted to stitch my wounds
with flames, burn the flesh until
I saw the God that I don't think
hears prayers or anything else.

Unfolding the maps, I wonder
how to navigate to a home
where my loved ones shared
beds, cotton blankets, warmth.

Turning wine into vinegar
is a miracle of time: My mother
told me Abraham answered
the call of fire, announcing
his present to presence
like a poorly painted target
for a well-hewn crossbow bolt.

The exhaustion comes like
the binding of a child's feet;
one looks for a ram out
of the corner of the eye
or hoping that one forget
the knife. I remember
Mother's cigarette shining

in the dark of the living
room. I hoped I would stand
above the glittering world,
the elastic hem of my pajamas
caught on the sky, my wings
melting because the Greeks,
my dreams don't understand
physics, but the distances of dreams

don't solve the equations. I am here,
and time arrives with eyes darker
than mine, and desert sand trapped
in glass shaped like a woman's silhouette.
It's hard not to be sentimental about red
algae blooms in the ocean, coloring
the sea wine-dark with the bodies
of fish. I don't pray, I know fire
makes the ashes, but the dust
only comes with time. Mud-packed
into the cataplasm I placed
on the throbbing, broken flesh.

Making Love to the Sounds of a Televised War

"A time is coming when men will go mad, and when they see someone who is not mad, they will attack him,
saying, 'You are mad; you are not like us.'"
—St. Anthony the Great

Feels like loss,
like losing
blood mixed
with storm water.
My body contorts
like a tightened
rope, her
pubis rubs

my chest
as my throat freezes
like a tundra choked
in heath, dressed
in permafrost, or
like the desert

of Saint Anthony
under caresses of
the Sun, whose
touch aged
his face like
smoked camel

hide. In my chest,
I feel Anthony's
door being opened,
inviting the demons
that would pick

at his tanned
flesh, arranging
each assault
with the arsenal
available
in such heat.

Anthony lay,
half-encrusted
in the sand, spent.

In the mumble
of a dead anchorite:
A missile
hits a Baghdad
hotel. The apocalypse,
afterglow, revealing,
reveling, the hum
of a helicopter lost.

Splinters from Crooked Timber

A red-breasted robin   lurks on grating
    above the lime   tree in the garden.   My
two cats bask   under a basil bush and in the
heat,   I wonder if the world   is real, even
    if I know   I am.

II.

The Night   confuse sentimental   and
     sentinel,   I hurl myself through
a new city, medieval stone streets   near neon lights
     in the distance. Capillary foot paths
which I fly by   like some drone   into forgetful
     history. I wonder about a date I had in Manhattan
a woman with a penchant for hip melancholy
     of drunk poets,   but also a fantasy
for handsome anarchists   in Brooklyn bars.
     Who is watching this?

We see things as we believe: pink blurs on blue sky
       I can't remember, and   no one can make me
Remember.   Waking with a beautiful   friend at two a.m.
         In San Francisco   ambling toward Chinatown
A man   yells   *Your boyfriend is a chump.*   The burn
    Is like   vodka, my fists clinch.   *Ignore him.*
The usual male ache   to thrust   to win   to prove.

IV.

By the time I awoke,   I knew a man who taught
    Poker was devotion   to a God who plays dice,
But his eyes yellowed   like the edges of a book
After too much gin   infused with meaning.
      Across from a strip mall,   a small family
Cemetery is choked   with kudzu and June bugs.

Windblown   I have trouble containing myself   When it's
        Time to move   I think I may rise   against the thistle burr
And into collision   with more   pieces of wood
            I have avoided   shaving   and cutting
Away   Why have we came
        Why can I not avoid   the heat of the pronoun
As if I am avoiding   someone   already dead.

VI.

      Three great   abstract loves   truth   beauty
History   it is a shame   they all hate   each other
Despite   a prolonged history of   making out
    History is   particularly good   at seducing one
To hate fucking when you kiss   it,   you can taste
        Heat   but also ice and bone

Yir'eh Shalem   someone says   means "we shall see peace"
    More than a bit   ironic   like the new angel
Walter Benjamin saw   falling against the   wind of history
But we forget   that angels are six-winged   monsters
    That speak for a void   with their four heads   with voices
That damage   We know there   are monsters in heaven
    We know this   like we know there
    Are monsters invisibly living   in dust
As the mites eat   our dead skin

VIII.

We move away   from the physical world
               From this tree of life   no straight thing is made
There are corpses of June bugs   in winter frost   there
Is rot   in the pines   where did you sleep last night
               In some field   amongst the dirt
Amongst the graves   that feed us all

The smear of white chalk
on a forgotten notebook.
Near the Mexican gold poppies
and Cascalote Trees, where

I go to sulk in the warmth
of noon sun, I watch a witch
moth hide in the shade. The words
tighten in the heat around

the throat. The moth dust
glitters my shirt. Fifteen years
ago, my aunt died on the highway
in the middle of a sunny day.

The sky hangs like wet crepe
paper. My aunt's hand
was palsied from AIDS. Body
turned against her, but a blinded

truck driver did the deed. Now
it's time for the Sun to pay as
I draw the moon over and over
on age-creamed paper. The

moth will follow me home,
cling to the events and die
an aristocrat's death. I want
for the cool darkness, my ally,

who aids in stuffing away
the sunlight when the quota
is met. I never saw my cousin
cry, but I avoid funerals. I'd

rather forget the mannequin
make-up and forced smiles.
I'd rather draw the stars of
dreams, words garroting

the last of the poems out
of my memory. I will sit
here staring at a soon-to-be
dead moth as the

cooling white hot star
solidifies akin to hope.

Pornography is boring
like watching someone
chew steak for twenty
minutes. Lacking all
context: the smell
of cherry blossoms
and sweat, the years
of watching someone
read Milton and not
become a misogynist,
the flannel nightgowns
or their lack.

To speak of bodies, to ask
we to come to bed with *us*
after a Fellini film or
complaining about Spielberg
or in the pauses between
breaths. Loving more

than the pulse, the twitch
of flesh. Consciousness
between people is too
bright. Gibbous light.
Half-reflected. Swelling.
What we wanted from
two or three, what we
want from one. Glacier
slow and churning
like salt slush between
a tow line.

To speak of love, to ask
of every cliché that it lingers
into strangeness, like filming
a crystal wine glass until
it looks like mountains
of barren, jagged
materials.

Erosion 5

To be beautiful is to learn
to fight with an open fist:
make-up is a war-paint.
Pecans darken in wet

fall grass, and we can
make out the ghosts
with dyed red hair,
whose breath smells

of bourbon. There is
no audience here, a love
of landscape moves beyond
her face. The countryside

wrinkles and unwrinkles
in the grasslands. Outside
renunciation, I am dregs
of absolute being. Ugliness

is skin deep, beauty is the
symmetrical application
of delusion. Good geometry
can change your life: forever

joined, forever apart like a
nut split and the shell discarded.
In the end it rains men and women—
Unforsaken, insolent, naked.

Displacement: Migrations

What is the price of two sparrows:
the schedule of trains left ripped
on the bedside. The dates past,
leaving little, not even laughter.

Staring at the aloe in the garden
you see the ridges, serrating the
air between, the cooling pulp
invisible, the soft inner-shadow

of wound. Spread over the burn
like butter, twisting the pain into
a kindness, granting no credential
but coolness to the touch. Dry air.

II.

The garden of ghosts: staking
out my position near a food
stand. I watch a small Mexican
boy run after a smaller flock

of pigeons, iridescent tips to
their wings like burning oil
on water, cutting the sky until
the boy is clear in my vision.

I smile for the first time in days:
the boy terrorizing the birds
of the hour, joy at the price
of escaping pigeon's peace.

Erosion 6

For the kindness of women and unkindness of time

What time is it? Could you take
me home to the chewed-on book edges
and unshaved armpits? I doubt
you have the time. The shock will come.

The paper is ripped on the page
of my favorite Alejandra Pizarnik
poem, my ear aches, and I cool
my hand with a glass of anything

hard and cheap. New Year's in
Seoul, soon to be divorced, already
long estranged, the wind chills my blood.
Home is where the head isn't.

The whisky wrapped in meat
and bone, I try chatting with
a blonde, but the conversation
might as well long march into

the next March. Time slips in
these poems, collapsing in from
New Year to New Year. Now
I am in the Mexican desert

wandering among the agave
and sun spiders, conversing
with *chanates* in the cold, clear
sky. Running out of mescal,

run back to the expat Seoul bar,
and I try to fall into her arms.
*Can you be so kind as to take
me home?* I am lost, and so

is she. She falls on ice in
tights, soju drunk. Coherence,
her hair dyed red, she speaks
slurred Cebuano and apologizes.

Later, I see the bruises on her legs
as she changes. You want a love story:
I slept on the floor and watched her
sleep. The next morning we talked

around the tiny apartment littered
with boxes, the skeleton of her life.
In confusion, everyone's *darling* but
I don't know these buildings. I don't

know where the space between space
and time lies. The December ritual only
does so much when I think I am lost.
The desert wind is cold, the oceans

travel. Home is where the good enough
sleep, together and alone. Across the Bay,
I am in California in a hotel crying with
another she. The ruins on the beach

in the cool winter, the so-called edge
of continent, but we know it all erodes
and bleeds to the beneath. *Would you
be kind enough to take me home?* The

venomous soft jelly stings long after
being dead. The undersides. Memory
in the purest hue of gray, unwinking.
The *chanate's* chatter distracts as I lie

on the tile, out of mescal, mercy. In
the distance the sky rumbles—far-off
fireworks or gunshots. Take. Me.

Variations on the Scrawl of Light

**I.   "For you are my lamp, O Lord,
and my God lightens my darkness" —2 Samuel 22: 29**

For several days the visitors
stayed, the foliar fading in
callused light thick in panes
frosting opaque, and bright

enough to break the stone,
mortar, brick that houses
each of our slithering
consciousnesses. The

promise of winter crystallizes,
we have a hard time believing
that we'll lack each other,
but ice and snow blinds

enough to keep the dark
things away, and keep our
days in which we suffer
much more light than heat.

II.   Hinc lucem et pocula sacra.

In the sour of our blood
there is a bitter humor,
we laughed at shadow
puppets of copulating

birds. Flight as fingers
fingering the obscene
in blocked light. The
present is a husk, kept

empty so that anything
can break like a fissure
in a dream light endowed.
Slate roofs cast a silver

hue which is ironic in
utter darkness of closed
eyes, enigmatic is the syntax
of light—the pinpricks that
pock the dark softening. By

small effort, the tiny holes
ooze heat which rises from
reflection off of water on
fresh green grass. What

vision promises in the last
scattering surfaces? Even
in the cheap seats we can
see the way shadows fall.

III. **"Corruption springs from light: 'tis one same power." —Philip James Bailey**

Through the bus window
I see the trash-haulers bring
me their dark. Traffic spectral
in half-night liquefies the air

in browning sky: the metallic
taste coats the tongue as two
chocolate bars stain my teeth.
At the bus I stared down strangers,

hoping that I was never there
and challenging each to prove
me. The Book of Nature is riddled
with errors and lesser gestures:

This pox we don't wish to see,
to examine, to cut into discrete
truths like scissoring away the edges
and blurring. Darkness hides

the leathery woman who slowly
picks up the trash. The heart is not
beautiful: clotted with fats and beating
blood into submission. The angry

meth-addled man apes a sexual
motion as if fucking the air
itself. Light lacks grace, lacks
even the silence of street wisdom.

IV. **"And the light shineth in darkness; and the darkness comprehended it not. "**
   —John 1:5

The angle of vision—
mud bricks before
a broken face from
falling, moon shuttering

in the haze reflected
in wet concrete to be
darkened with blood,
but cutting away the

scene illuminates again
fluid thickened flashes
in fear and oaths of
stone and gravel.

V.   "Love is not consolation. It is light." —Friedrich Nietzsche

Exception spines the boundary:
this you can't see. Days are counted
by two-dimensional cutting, demarcations
of vision. This light, a stabbing.

Inward. There is no deadline
to the perception. No heaven
left by the violence of a punch
line. The sky is vast, cold, and,

in all things, bright. Glories
surround the vision, glories
illuminate the mountains of
Baekje through the airplane:

glories, halos of evanescent
waves coupling. This light,
a cup. Holding inward
like sucking in air after

a kiss. Bring me a small
detail. Bring me bright.

Erosion 7

Wet dreams about Mary Poppins
erupt and burst in boyhood, Julie
Andrews's face guiding me to rituals
of dull caprice. The rest of this I hid:

you don't understand. Comedic my
self-control: sometimes I say too much.
Let the *is* speak for itself: times when I
was with you, I was really not myself

but I didn't want the truth; with each
new scenario, we kept the joking coming.
Chosen for and chosen by the elect
clamoring for some new heaven, erected

like cars rutting on summer asphalt. Between
the birthmark and the stain, you became
so many people. Mary Poppins's sugared
spoons no longer have the erotic tinge:

you who wish to control the pain,
the gout in your metaphors, the shattered
tooth leaving splinters. For unburdening,
I will not kneel and grotesque, I will undress

watching my hairs gray, shadowing the wounds.
We will not certify our pains: I have longed for
you, desire gone away. Feel the yammering

at the mouth, it is your turn, beloved ghost,
there are emotions to be overwritten and songs
to be unsung. Another woman will sleep with me,
and probably another with you. I have said it

all, and the wall between our past and our fading
abrades against the sand. But what a hope,
neither starved nor cold. The autumn cherry
blossoms fall in romantic decadence, we

deliberately muddy the imaging. The pollen
chokes the sky green and yellow, you pull another
gray hair out of my stubble. In that moment, we touched
and nothing could be said. Age, my mask,

it's your turn. I hear Julie Andrew's whispers.

Grace

We start work of philosophy composed
entirely of jokes, the philosopher
giggles to himself as he shrinks
back into his naïve tweed. We pretend

we get it: You are here. A dot
on a map. In the cartographies
of the future, you are still a dot,
and you will think of her as a train

goes by, speeding toward the edge
of the map. To make a woman laugh,
I would undo the knot at the base
of the stomach, lead the eyes to

heavily lift, cause a smile to palpitate
into small, subtle breaths. You stand
at the exit—flirting is funny, but
wonder at the punch line. I would

photograph you smiling under
the red light an evacuation sign.
The map didn't mention it. Some
gag, you think. You hold your

hand out to mine, ricocheting
off the edges of the legend. To know
a woman trusts me: opens
up the rib cage splaying with

delicate scalpel, causing more
dots smeared on the typography.
My smile lingers a bit too long;
in the cavity of my chest, you

pack the sinew thick with mud,
loosely form a heart to grow
lilacs and small, sweet berries.
With dirty hands, you giggle.

Afterword: On What Cannot Be Said

A fly lands   green metallic
eyes and all   on a corpse
what is not to be loved

the moment for antennae
the slide over hairs still
brown on gray skin

the beauty here beyond
the context   beyond the
text   beyond the given
language   each blue
sky blue   sky blush
sky bluer   you can

see but not speak of
and if I do not tell you
or if I cannot   you will
not   know   the car wreck

on I-75 or the old man
whose second stroke brought
him down or the boy
stabbed   four times with
a wet kitchen knife no

even if you did know   I
could not tell you any more
I could not encapsulate

a life or even the hum
of a fly's wings if you
have not already heard

C. Derick Varn is a poet and teacher now living in Salt Lake City. He works for Zero Books as a reader of theory and nonfiction and is a poetry reviewer for the *Hong Kong Review of Books*. He serves as a podcast co-host and co-producer for *Symptomatic Redness* and *Alternatives*. He co-founded and edits the online literary journal, *Former People*.

Derick has spent most of the last decade abroad: first in South Korea, then in Northern Mexico, and Egypt. He traveled with his wife through Asia, Turkey, and Mexico in his off-time as well as studies history of socialism and alternative political movements.

Poems in this collection have appeared in *JMWW; The Toronto Quarterly; Unlikely Stories; Former People: A Journal of Bangs and Whimpers; The Writing Disorder; Union Station; Yes, Poetry!; The Axe Factory; Unscene;* and *Streetcake Magazine*.

Thanks to my primary readers for the various versions of this manuscript that I have had in the past decade and who helped me whittle it into its current form: Martin Lammon, Laura Newbern, Oni Buchanan, Alice Friman, Miller Oberman, Elizabeth Fogle, Cindy Hochman, and Jonathan Penton.

Special thanks to my wife, Khristian Owens.

Recent Titles from Unlikely Books

My Hands Were Clean by Tom Bradley (Second Edition)

We'll See Who Seduces Whom by Tom Bradley

_a ship on the line by Vincent A. Cellucci and Christopher Shipman

Scorpions by Joel Chace

Love and Other Lethal Things by K. R. Copeland

Soy solo palabras but wish to be a city by Leon De la Rósa and Gui.ra.ga7 (Second Edition)

ANCHOR WHAT by Vernon Frazer

Definitions of Obscurity by Vernon Frazer and Michelle Greenblatt (Second Edition of *Dark Hope*, Argotist E-Books)

ASHES AND SEEDS by Michelle Greenblatt

brain : storm by Michelle Greenblatt (Second Edition, originally anabasis Press)

pleth by j/j hastain and Marthe Reed

anonymous gun. by Kurtice Kucheman (Second Edition)

Monolith by Anne McMillen (Second Edition)

When Red Blood Cells Leak by Anne McMillen (Second Edition)

Ghazals 1-59 and Other Poems by Sheila E. Murphy and Michelle Greenblatt

#specialcharacters by Larissa Shmailo

Blue Rooms, Black Holes, White Lights by Belinda Subraman (Second Edition)

Beautiful Rush by Marc Vincenz

Gods of a Ransacked Century by Marc Vincenz

Pachuco Skull with Sombrero, Los Angeles 1970 by Lawrence Welsh

23144737R00062

Made in the USA
Columbia, SC
06 August 2018